Family Worship

FAMILY GUIDANCE SERIES
By Joel R. Beeke

The church must maintain the divinely ordered role of the family to establish a godly heritage. In this ongoing series, Dr. Joel R. Beeke offers pastoral insight and biblical direction for building strong Christian families.

Books in the series:
Bringing the Gospel to Covenant Children
Family Worship
The Family at Church

Family Worship

Joel R. Beeke

REFORMATION HERITAGE BOOKS
Grand Rapids, Michigan

Family Worship
© 2002, 2009 by Joel R. Beeke

Published by
Reformation Heritage Books
2965 Leonard St., NE
Grand Rapids, MI 49525
616-977-0889/Fax 616-285-3246
e-mail: orders@heritagebooks.org
website: www.heritagebooks.org

Printed in the United States of America
14 15 16 17 18 19/12 11 10 9 8 7 6

Library of Congress Cataloging-in-Publication Data

Beeke, Joel R., 1952-
  Family worship / Joel R. Beeke.
      p. cm. — (Family guidance series)
  Includes bibliographical references and index.
  ISBN 978-1-60178-058-4 (pbk. : alk. paper)
  1. Family—Religious life. I. Title.
  BV4526.3.B44 2009
  249—dc22

                                         2008054841

---

*For additional Reformed literature request
a free book list from the above address.*

With gratitude to

Lydia Ruth Beeke

my beautiful, soft-spoken daughter,
tender-hearted before God and man;
my detailed artist, star speller,
and competitive Uno player;
congratulations on entering your teen years!

May God one day bless you with a
God-fearing home that thrives on family worship.

Soli Deo Gloria!

Contents

Theological Foundations of Family Worship

1

Every church desires growth. Surprisingly few churches, however, seek to promote internal church growth by stressing the need to raise children in covenantal truth. Few seriously grapple with why many adolescents become nominal members with mere notional faith or abandon evangelical truth for unbiblical doctrine and modes of worship.

I believe one major reason for this failure is the lack of stress upon family worship. In many churches and homes family worship is an optional thing, or at most a superficial exercise such as a brief table grace before meals. Consequently, many children grow up with no experience or impression of Christian faith and worship as a daily reality. When my parents commemorated their fiftieth anniversary, all five of us children decided to express thanks to our father and mother for one thing without consulting each other. Remarkably, all five of us thanked our mother for her prayers and all five of us thanked our father for his leadership of our Sunday evening family worship.

My brother said, "Dad, the oldest memory I have is of tears streaming down your face as you taught us from *Pilgrim's Progress* on Sunday evenings how the Holy Spirit leads believers. At the age of three God used you in family worship to convict me that Christianity was real. No matter how far I went astray in later years, I could never seriously question the reality of Christianity, and I want to thank you for that."

Would we see revival among our children? Let us remember that God often uses the restoration of family worship to usher in church revival. For example, the 1677 church covenant of the Puritan congregation in Dorchester, Massachusetts, included the commitment "to reform our families, engaging ourselves to a conscientious care to set before us and to maintain the worship of God in them; and to walk in our houses with perfect hearts in a faithful discharge of all domestic duties, educating, instructing, and charging our children and households to keep the ways of the Lord."[1]

As goes the home, so goes the church, so goes the nation. Family worship is a most decisive factor in how the home goes.

Family worship is not the only factor, of course. Family worship is not a substitute for other parental

1. Leland Ryken, *Worldly Saints: The Puritans As They Really Were* (Grand Rapids: Zondervan, 1986), p. 80. Cf. Horton Davies, "Puritan Family Worship," in *The Worship of the English Puritans* (Glasgow: Dacre Press, 1948), pp. 278–85; Jerry Marcellino, *Rediscovering the Lost Treasure of Family Worship* (Laurel, Miss.: Audubon Press, 1996), pp. 1–3.

duties. Family worship without parental example is futile. Spontaneous teaching that arises throughout a typical day is crucial, yet set times of family worship are also important. Family worship is the foundation of biblical child-rearing.

In this booklet, we will examine family worship under five headings: (1) theological foundations, (2) duty; (3) implementation; (4) objections; (5) motivation.

The theological foundations of family worship are rooted in the very being of God. The apostle John tells us that God's love is inseparable from His triune life. God's love is outgoing and overflowing. It shares its blessedness from one Person of the Trinity to the others. God has never been a solitary individual lacking something in Himself. The fullness of light and love is eternally shared among the Father, Son, and Spirit.

The majestic triune God didn't model Himself after our families; rather, He modeled the earthly concept of family after Himself. Our family life faintly reflects the life of the Holy Trinity. That's why Paul speaks of "the Father of our Lord Jesus Christ, of whom the family in heaven and earth is named" (Eph. 3:14–15). The love among the persons of the Trinity was so great from eternity that the Father determined to create a world of people who, though finite, would have personalities that reflected the Son. Being conformed to the Son, people could then share in the blessed holiness and joy of the Trinity's family life.

God created Adam in His own image, and Eve from Adam. From them came the entire human family so that mankind might have covenantal fellowship with God. As a two-person family, our first parents reverently worshiped God as He walked with them in the garden of Eden (Gen. 3:8).

Adam disobeyed God, however, turning the joy of worship and fellowship with God into fear, dread, guilt, and alienation. As our representative, Adam severed the relationship between the family of God and the family of mankind. But God's purpose could not be thwarted. While they yet stood before Him in Paradise, God held forth a new covenant, the covenant of grace, and told Adam and Eve about His Son, who as the Seed of the woman would break the power of Satan over them, and secure to them the blessings of this covenant of grace (Gen. 3:15). Through Christ's obedience to the law and His sacrifice for sin, God opened the way to save sinners while satisfying His perfect justice. The Lamb would be slain on Golgotha to take away the sin of the world, so that poor sinners like us could be restored to our true purpose: to glorify, worship, and have fellowship with the triune God. As 1 John 1:3 says, "Truly our fellowship is with the Father, and with his Son Jesus Christ."

God deals with the human race through covenant and headship, or representation. In daily life, parents represent children, a father represents his wife and children, church officebearers represent church members, and legislators represent citizens. In spiritual life, every person is represented by either the first or the last Adam (see Romans 5 and 1 Corinthians 15). This principle of representation surfaces everywhere in Scripture. For example, we read of the godly line of Seth, and of Noah and Job offering sacrifices on their children's behalf (Gen. 8:20–21; Job 1:5). God organized the human race through families and tribes, and dealt largely with them through the headship of the father. As God said to Abraham, "In thee shall all families of the earth be blessed" (Gen. 12:3).

The Mosaic economy continued the principle of the father representing the family in worship and fellowship with God. The book of Numbers particularly focuses on God's dealing with His people in terms of families and their heads. The father was to lead the family in Passover worship and instruct his children in its meaning.

The father's leadership role in worship continued throughout the monarchy in Israel and in the days of the Old Testament prophets. For example, Zechariah predicted that as the Holy Spirit was poured out in a future age, the people would experience Him as the Spirit of grace and supplication, moving them, family by family, to bitter and heartfelt lamentation. Particular families are named according to their heads and fathers, the house of David, of Levi, and of Shimei (Zech. 12:10–14).

The relationship between worship and family life continued in New Testament times. Peter reaffirmed the promise to Abraham, the father of the faithful (Rom. 4:11), when he declared to the Jews in his Pentecost sermon that "the promise is unto you and to your children, and to all that are afar off" (Acts 2:39). And Paul tells us in 1 Corinthians 7:14 that the faith of a parent establishes the covenant status of holiness, privilege, and responsibility for his or her children. The New Testament church, which included children with their parents as members of the body (Eph. 6:1–4), and the experience of individual believers such as Timothy (2 Tim. 1:5, 3:15), affirm the importance of faith and worship within families.

As Douglas Kelly concludes, "Family religion, which depends not a little on the household head daily leading the family before God in worship, is one of the most powerful structures that the covenant-keeping God has given for the expansion of redemption through the generations, so that countless multitudes may be brought into communion with and worship" of the living God in the face of Jesus Christ.[2]

---

2. "Family Worship: Biblical, Reformed, and Viable for Today," in *Worship in the Presence of God*, ed. Frank J. Smith and David C. Lachman (Greenville, S.C.: Greenville Seminary Press, 1992), p. 110. Most of this last section is a condensed version of Douglas Kelly's excellent summary.

The Duty of Family Worship 2

Given the importance of family worship as a potent force in winning untold millions to gospel truth throughout the ages, we ought not be surprised that God requires heads of households do all they can to lead their families in worshiping the living God. Joshua 24:14–15 says, "Now therefore fear the LORD, and serve him in sincerity and in truth: and put away the gods which your fathers served on the other side of the flood, and in Egypt; and serve ye the LORD. And if it seem evil unto you to serve the LORD, choose you this day whom ye will serve; whether the gods which your fathers served that were on the other side of the flood [i.e. back in Ur of Chaldees], or the gods of the Amorites, in whose land ye dwell [i.e. here in Canaan]: but as for me and my house, we will serve the LORD."

Notice three things in this text: First, Joshua did not make worship or service to the living God optional. In verse 14, he has just commanded Israel to fear the Lord. In verse 15 he now stresses that the

Lord wills to be worshiped and served voluntarily and deliberately in our families.

Second, in verse 15, Joshua enforces the service of God in families with his own example. Verse 1 makes plain that he is addressing the heads of households. Verse 15 declares that Joshua is going to do what he wants every other household in Israel to do: "serve the LORD." Joshua has such command over his family that he speaks for the entire household: "as for me and my house, we will serve the LORD," he says. Several factors reinforce this bold declaration:

- When Joshua makes this declaration, he is more than 100 years old. He has remarkable zeal as an aged man.

- Joshua knows that his direct control over his family will soon end. God has told him he will soon die. Yet Joshua is confident that his influence will continue in his family and that they will not abandon worship after he dies.

- Joshua knows that much idolatry remains in Israel. He has just told the people to put away false gods (v. 14). He knows his family will be swimming against the stream in continuing to serve the Lord—yet he emphatically declares that his family will do that anyway.

- The historical record shows that Joshua's influence was so pervasive that most of the nation followed his example for at least one generation.

Joshua 24:31 says, "And Israel served the LORD all the days of Joshua, and all the days of the elders that overlived Joshua [i.e. for the next generation], and which had known all the works of the LORD, that he had done for Israel." What an encouragement to God-fearing parents to know that the worship they set up in the home may last generations after them!

Third, the word *serve* in verse 15 is an inclusive word. It is translated as *worship* many times in Scripture. The original word not only includes serving God in every sphere of our lives, but also in *special acts of worship*. Those who interpret Joshua's words in vague, ambiguous terms miss that critical teaching. Joshua had several things in mind, including obedience to all the ceremonial laws involving the sacrificing of animals and pointing to the coming Messiah, whose blood sacrifice would be effectual for sinners, once and for all.[1]

Surely every God-fearing husband, father, and pastor must say with Joshua: "As for me and my household, we will serve the Lord. We will seek the Lord, worship Him, and pray to Him as a family. We will read His Word, replete with instructions, and reinforce its teachings in our family." Every representative father must realize, as Kelly says, "The

---

1. James Hufstetler, *Family Worship: Practical Directives for Heads of Families* (Grand Rapids: Truth for Eternity Ministries, 1995), pp. 4–7.

representative principle inherent in God's covenant dealings with our race indicates that the head of each family is to represent his family before God in divine worship and that the spiritual atmosphere and long term personal welfare of that family will be affected in large measure by the fidelity—or failure—of the family head in this area."[2]

According to Scripture, God should be served in special acts of worship in families today in the following three ways:

(1) *Daily instruction in the Word of God.* God should be worshiped by daily reading and instruction from His Word. Through questions, answers, and instructions, parents and children are to daily interact with each other about sacred truth. As Deuteronomy 6:6–7 says, "And these words, which I command thee this day, shall be in thine heart: and thou shalt teach them diligently unto thy children, and shalt talk of them when thou sittest in thine house, and when thou walkest by the way, and when thou liest down, and when thou risest up" (cf. Deut. 11:18–19).

The activities this text commands are *daily* activities that accompany lying down at night, rising up in the morning, sitting in the house, and walking by the way. In an orderly home, these activities are done at specific times of the day. They offer opportunities for regular, consistent, and daily times of instruction.

---

2. *Worship in the Presence of God*, p. 112.

Moses wasn't suggesting a little talk, but diligent conversation and diligent instruction that flow from the burning heart of a parent. Moses says that words from God should be in a father's *heart*. Fathers must *diligently* teach these words to their children.

A parallel text in the New Testament is Ephesians 6:4, "And, ye fathers, provoke not your children to wrath: but bring them up in the nurture and admonition [i.e. instruction] of the Lord." When fathers cannot fulfil this duty in person, they should encourage their wives to carry out this precept. For example, Timothy benefited greatly from the daily instruction of a God-fearing mother and a God-fearing grandmother.

(2) *Daily prayer to the throne of God.* Jeremiah 10:25 says, "Pour out thy fury upon the heathen that know thee not, and upon the families that call not on thy name." While it is true that in the context of Jeremiah 10:25, the word *families* refers to clans, this word also applies to individual families. We may reason from larger units to smaller units. If God's wrath falls upon clans or groups of families that neglect communal prayer, how much more will not His wrath fall upon individual families that refuse to call on His name? All families must call upon God's name or else subject themselves to the displeasure of God.

Families must daily pray together unless providentially hindered. Consider Psalm 128:3, "Thy wife shall be as a fruitful vine by the sides of thine house:

thy children like olive plants round about thy table."
Families eat and drink the daily provision of a gracious God at their tables. To do that in a Christian
way, a family must follow 1 Timothy 4:4–5, "For every
creature of God is good, and nothing to be refused, if
it be received with thanksgiving: for it is sanctified
by the word of God and prayer." If you want to eat
and drink to the glory of God (1 Cor. 10:31), and the
food you are about to eat is to be set apart for that
purpose, you must sanctify it by prayer, Paul says.
And just as we pray the food and drink may be sanctified and blessed to the nourishment of our bodies,
so we should pray for God's blessing of His Word to
the nourishment of our souls. "Man shall not live by
bread alone but by every word that proceedeth from
the mouth of God" (Deut. 8:3; Matt. 4:4).

Furthermore, don't families commit daily sins?
Shouldn't they daily seek forgiveness? Does not God
bless them in many ways every day? Should not these
blessings be acknowledged with daily thanksgiving?
Shouldn't they daily acknowledge God in all their
ways, begging Him to direct their paths? Shouldn't
they daily commend themselves to His care and
protection? As Thomas Brooks said, "A family without prayer is like a house without a roof, open and
exposed to all the storms of heaven."

(3) *Daily singing the praise of God.* Psalm 118:15
says, "The voice of rejoicing and salvation is in the
tabernacles of the righteous: the right hand of the

LORD doeth valiantly." That is a clear reference to singing. The psalmist says this sound *is* (not simply *ought to be*) in the tents of the righteous. Philip Henry, father of the famed Matthew Henry, believed this text provided a biblical basis for the singing of psalms in families. He argued that joyful singing comes from the individual tents of the righteous. It involves family singing as well as temple singing. Therefore, the sound of rejoicing and salvation should rise from family homes on a daily basis.

Psalm 66:1–2 speaks similarly, "Make a joyful noise unto God, all ye lands: Sing forth the honour of his name: make his praise glorious." Here the duty of praising God in song is laid upon all lands, all nations, all families, all persons. Secondly, our songs are to be the psalms given by inspiration of God which show forth the honor of His Name—the verb "sing forth" (*zamar*) being the root of the word "psalm" (*mizmor*), and elsewhere translated, "sing psalms" (Ps. 105:2; cf. Jas. 5:13). Thirdly, we are to praise Him in a worthy manner, with a loud voice (2 Chron. 20:19), and with grace in the heart (Col. 3:16), so making His praise glorious.

The Lord is to be worshiped daily by the singing of psalms. God is glorified, and families are edified. Because these songs are God's Word, singing them is a means of instruction, enlightening the understanding. Singing promotes devotion as it warms the heart. The graces of the Spirit are stirred up in us, and our growth in grace is stimulated. "Let the word of Christ dwell in you richly in all wisdom; teaching and admonishing one another in psalms and hymns and spiritual songs, singing with grace in your hearts to the Lord" (Col. 3:16).

Heads of households, we must implement family worship in the home. God requires that we worship Him not only privately as individuals, but publicly as members of the covenant body and community, and socially, as families. The Lord Jesus is worthy of it, God's Word commands it, and conscience affirms it as our duty.

Our families owe their allegiance to God. God has placed us in a position of authority to guide our children in the way of the Lord. We are more than friends and advisors to our children; as their teacher and ruler in the home, our example and leadership are crucial. Clothed with holy authority, we owe to our children prophetical teaching, priestly intercession, and royal guidance (see Heidelberg Catechism, Q. 32). We must direct family worship by way of Scripture, prayer, and song.[3]

Those of us who are pastors, must lovingly inform the heads of families in our churches that they must command their household to worship God as Abraham did. "For I know him," God said, "that he will *command* his children and his household after him, and

---

3. Oliver Heywood, "Family Worship A Commanded Duty: An Exhortation of Heads of Families," *The Banner of Truth,* No. 5 (Apr. 1957):36 – 40, and "The Family Altar," in *The Works of Oliver Heywood* (Morgan, Penn.: Soli Deo Gloria, 1999), 4:294 – 418.

they shall keep the way of the LORD, to do justice and judgment; that the LORD may bring upon Abraham that which he hath spoken of him" (Gen. 18:19).

Implementing Family Worship 3

Here are some suggestions to help you establish God-honoring family worship in your homes. We trust this avoids two extremes: an idealistic approach that is beyond the reach of even the most God-fearing home, and a minimalist approach that abandons daily family worship because the ideal seems so out of reach.

Prepare for Family Worship

Even before family worship begins, we should privately pray for God's blessing upon that worship. Then we should plan for the *what, where*, and *when* of family worship.

1. *What.* Generally speaking, this includes instruction in the Word of God, prayer before the throne of God, and singing to the glory of God. But we need to determine more of the specifics of family worship.

First, have Bibles and copies of *The Psalter* and song sheets for all the children who can read. For children who are too young to read, read a few verses from Scripture and select one text to memorize as a family. Say it aloud together several times as a family, then reinforce that with a short Bible story to illustrate the text. Take time to teach a stanza or two of a Psalter selection to such children, and encourage them to sing with you.

For young children, try using *Truths of God's Word,* which has a guide for teachers and parents that illustrates each doctrine. For children in grade four and up, try James W. Beeke's Bible Doctrine series with accompanying teachers' guides. Jeff Kingswood's *From the Lips of Little Ones* is another good resource. In any case, explain what you have read to your children, and ask them a question or two. Then sing one or two psalms and a sound hymn or a good chorus like "Dare to be a Daniel." Close with prayer.

For older children, read a passage from Scripture, memorize it together, then apply a proverb. Ask questions about how to apply those verses to daily life, or perhaps read a portion from the gospels and its corresponding section in J.C. Ryle's *Expository Thoughts on the Gospels.* Ryle is simple yet profound. His clear points help generate discussion. Perhaps you'd like to read parts of an inspirational biography. Don't let the reading of edifying literature replace Bible-reading or its application, however.

John Bunyan's *Pilgrim's Progress* or *Holy War,* or daily meditations by Charles Spurgeon are appropriate for more spiritually minded children. Older children will also benefit from *365 Days with Cal-*

vin, William Jay's *Morning and Evening Exercises*, William Mason's *Spiritual Treasury*, and Robert Hawker's *Poor Man's Morning and Evening Portions*. After those readings, sing a few familiar psalms and perhaps learn a new one before closing with prayer.

Use should also be made of the creeds and confessions of the church. Young children should be taught to say the Apostles' Creed and the Lord's Prayer. If you adhere to the Westminster standards, have your children memorize the Shorter Catechism over time. If the Heidelberg Catechism is preached in your congregation, read on Sabbath mornings the Lord's Day of the Catechism from which the minister will be preaching at church. If you have *The Psalter*, occasional use can be made of the forms of devotion found in *Christian Prayers*.[1] Using these forms at home will afford opportunity for you and your children to learn to use such forms in an edifying and profitable manner, a skill which will stand you all in good stead when the liturgical forms are used as part of public worship.

2. *Where.* Family worship may be held around the supper table; however, it might be better to move to the living room, where there are fewer distractions.

---

1. Pp. 169–178. See especially forms for "Prayer before Meals" and "Thanksgiving after Meals" (pp. 173–74), and "Morning Prayer" and "Evening Prayer" (pp. 175–76).

Whatever room you select, make sure it contains all of your devotional materials. Before you start, take the phone off the hook, or plan to let your answering machine or voice mail take messages. Your children must understand that family worship is the most important activity of the day and should not be interrupted by anything.

3. *When*. Ideally, family worship should be conducted twice a day, in the morning and in the evening. That fits best with scriptural directions for worship—both the Old Testament economy in which the beginning and close of each day were sanctified by the offering of morning and evening sacrifices as well as morning and evening prayers, and the New Testament church which apparently followed the pattern of morning and evening prayers. The Westminster Directory of Worship states, "Family worship, which ought to be performed by every family, *ordinarily morning and evening*, consists in prayer, reading the Scriptures, and singing praises."[2]

For some families, family worship is scarcely possible more than once a day, after the evening meal. Either way, heads of households must be sensitive to the family schedule and keep everyone involved. Practice the principle of Matthew 6:33 ("Seek ye

---

2. *Westminster Confession of Faith* (Glasgow: Free Presbyterian Publications, 1976), pp. 419–20.

first the kingdom of God, and his righteousness") in establishing a family schedule.

Carefully guard this time of family worship. If you know ahead of time that the normal time will not be suitable on a certain day, reschedule worship time. Don't skip it, however; that can become habitual. When you can keep to your appointed times, plan carefully and prepare beforehand to make every minute count. Fight every enemy of family worship.

During Family Worship

During family worship, aim for the following:

1. *Brevity*. As Richard Cecil said, "Let family worship be short, savory, simple, tender, heavenly." Family worship that is too long makes children restless and may provoke them to wrath.

If you worship twice a day, try ten minutes in the morning and a little longer in the evening. A twenty-five minute period of family worship might be divided as follows: ten minutes for Scripture reading and instruction; five minutes for reading a daily portion or an edifying book or discussing some concern in a biblical light; five minutes for singing; and five minutes for prayer.

2. *Consistency*. It is better to have twenty minutes of family worship every day than to try for extended periods on fewer days—say forty-five minutes on Monday,

then skipping Tuesday. Family worship provides us "the manna which falls every day at the door of the tent, that our souls are kept alive," wrote James W. Alexander in his excellent book on family worship.[3]

Don't indulge excuses to avoid family worship. If you lost your temper at a child a half-hour before family worship time, don't say: It's hypocritical for me to lead family worship, so we'll skip it tonight. You don't need to run from God at such times. Rather, you must return to God like the penitent publican. Begin worship time by asking everyone who witnessed your loss of temper to forgive you, then pray to God for forgiveness. Children will respect you for that. They will tolerate weaknesses and even sins in their parents so long as the parents confess their wrongdoings and earnestly seek to follow the Lord. They and you know that the Old Testament high priest was not disqualified for being a sinner but had first to offer sacrifice for himself before he could offer sacrifices for the people's sins. Neither are you and I disqualified today for confessed sin, for our sufficiency lies in Christ, not in ourselves. As A. W. Pink said, "It is not the sins of a Christian, but his unconfessed sins, which choke the channel of blessing and cause so many to miss God's best."[4]

Lead family worship with a firm, fatherly hand

---

3. *Thoughts on Family Worship* (Philadelphia: Presbyterian Board of Publications, 1847), chap. 1.

4. *Pink's Jewels,* (MacDill, Florida: Tyndale Bible Society, n.d.), p. 91.

and a soft, penitent heart. Even when you're bone-weary after a day's work, pray for strength to carry out your fatherly duty. Remember that Christ Jesus went to the cross for you bone-weary and exhausted but never shrunk from His mission. As you deny yourself, you will see how He strengthens you during family worship, so that by the time you finish, your exhaustion is overcome.

3. *Hopeful solemnity.* "Rejoice with trembling before the Lord," Psalm 2 tells us. We need to show this balance of hope and awe, fear and faith, repentance and confidence in family worship. Speak naturally yet reverently during this time, using the tone you would use when speaking to a deeply respected friend about a serious matter. Expect great things from a great covenant-keeping God.

Let's get more specific:
1. For the reading of Scripture

* *Have a plan.* Read ten or twenty verses from the Old Testament in the morning and ten to twenty from the New Testament in the evening. Or read a series of parables, miracles, or biographical portions. For example, read 1 Kings 17 to 2 Kings 2 to study the prophet Elijah. Or follow a theme throughout Scripture. Wouldn't it be interesting, for example, to read the so-called "night scenes"—all the histories in Scripture that take place at night? Or to read portions of Scripture

that follow Christ's sufferings from His circumcision to His burial? Or to read a series of selections that highlight various attributes of God? Just be sure to read the entire Bible over a period of time. As J.C. Ryle said, "Fill their minds with Scripture. Let the Word dwell in them richly. Give them the Bible, the whole Bible, even while they are young."[5]

• *Account for special occasions.* On Sunday mornings you might want to read Psalm 48, 63, 84, 92, 118, or John 20. On the Sabbath when the Lord's Supper is to be administered, read Psalm 22, Isaiah 53, Matthew 26, or part of John 6. Before you leave home for family vacations, gather your family in the living room and read Psalm 91 or Psalm 121. When someone in the family is sick, read John 11. When someone is greatly distressed by a prolonged trial, read Isaiah 40–66. When a believer is dying, read Revelation 7, 21, and 22.

• *Involve the family.* Every family member who can read should have a Bible to follow along. Set the tone by reading Scripture with expression, as the living, "breathing" book it is. Assign various portions to be read by your wife and your children—including preschool children who cannot yet read. Take your 4 year-old on your lap and whisper a few words at a time into the child's ear,

---

5. *The Duties of Parents* (Conrad, Mont.: Triangle Press, 1993), p. 11.

and ask the child to repeat them aloud. One or two verses "read" in this manner is sufficient for a preschooler to feel included in the family Bible-reading. Older children could read four or five verses each, or you could assign the full reading to one child each day.

Teach your children how to read articulately and with expression. Don't let them mumble or speed ahead. Teach them to read with reverence. Provide a brief word of explanation throughout the reading, according to the needs of the younger children.

• *Encourage private Bible reading and study.* Be sure that you and your children close the day with the Word of God. You might follow Robert Murray M'Cheyne's *Calendar for Bible Readings* so that your children read the Bible on their own once each year. Help each child build a personal library of Bible-based books.

2. For biblical instruction
   • *Be plain in meaning.* Ask your children if they understand what you are reading. Be plain in applying scriptural texts. The 1647 Church of Scotland Directory provides counsel here:

   > The holy scriptures should be read ordinarily to the family; and it is commendable, that thereafter they confer, and by way of conference, make some good use of what hath been read and heard. As, for example, if any sin be

reproved in the word read, use may be made thereof to make all the family circumspect and watchful against the same; or if any judgment be threatened or mentioned to have been inflicted, in that portion of scripture which is read, use may be made to make all the family fear lest the same or a worse judgment befall them, unless they beware of the sin that procured it: and finally, if any duty be required, or comfort held forth in a promise, use may be made to stir up themselves to employ Christ for strength to enable them for doing the commanded duty, and to apply the offered comfort. In all which the master of the family is to have the chief hand; and any member of the family may propose a question or doubt for resolution (par. III).[6]

Encourage family dialogue around God's Word in line with the Hebraic procedure of household questions and answers (cf. Ex. 12; Deut. 6; Ps. 78). Especially encourage teenagers to ask questions; draw them out. If you don't know the answers, tell them so, and encourage them to search for answers. Have one or more good commentaries on hand, such as those by John Calvin, Matthew Poole, and Matthew Henry. Remember, if you don't provide answers for your

---

6. *Westminster Confession of Faith,* p. 419.

children, they will get them elsewhere—and often those will be wrong answers.

* *Be pure in doctrine.* Titus 2:7 says, "In all things showing thyself a pattern of good works: in doctrine showing uncorruptness, gravity, sincerity." Don't abandon doctrinal precision when teaching young children; aim for simplicity and soundness.

* *Be relevant in application.* Don't be afraid to share your experiences when appropriate, but do that simply. Use concrete illustrations. Ideally, tie together biblical instruction with what you recently heard in sermons.

* *Be affectionate in manner.* Proverbs continually uses the phrase "my son," showing the warmth, love, and urgency in the teachings of a God-fearing father. When you must administer the wounds of a father-friend to your children, do that with heartfelt love. Tell them you must convey the whole counsel of God because you can't bear the thought of spending eternity apart from them. My father often said to us, with tears: "Children, I cannot miss any of you in heaven." Tell your children: "We will allow you every privilege an open Bible will allow us to give you—but if we say no to you, you must know that flows out of our love." As Ryle said: "Love is one grand

secret of successful training. Soul love is the soul of all love."[7]

◆ *Require attention.* Proverbs 4:1 says, "Hear, ye children, the instruction of a father, and attend to know understanding." Fathers and mothers have important truths to convey. You must demand a hearing for God's truths in your home. That may involve repeated statements at the beginning like these: "Sit up, son, and look at me when I'm talking. We're talking about God's Word, and God deserves to be heard." Don't allow children to leave their seats during family worship, except for emergencies.

3. For praying

◆ *Be short.* With few exceptions, don't pray for more than five minutes. Tedious prayers do more harm than good.

Don't teach in your prayer; God doesn't need the instruction. Teach with your eyes open; pray with your eyes shut.

◆ *Be simple without being shallow.* Pray for things that your children know something about, but don't allow your prayers to become trivial. Don't reduce your prayers to self-centered, shallow petitions.

◆ *Be direct.* Spread your needs before God, plead

---

7. *The Duties of Parents,* p. 9.

your case, and ask for mercy. Name your teenagers and children and their needs one by one on a daily basis. That holds tremendous weight with them.

• *Be natural yet solemn.* Speak clearly and reverently. Don't use an unnatural, high-pitched voice or a monotone. Don't pray too loudly or softly, too fast or slow.

• *Be varied.* Don't pray the same thing every day; that becomes monotonous. Develop more variety in prayer by remembering and stressing the various ingredients of true prayer, such as:

Invocation, adoration, and dependence. Begin by mentioning one or two titles or attributes of God, such as, "Gracious and holy Lord...." To that add a declaration of your desire to worship God and your dependence upon Him for His assistance in prayer. For example, say: "We bow humbly in Thy presence—Thou who art worthy to be worshiped, praying that our souls may be lifted up to Thee. Assist us by Thy Spirit. Help us to call upon Thy Name by Jesus Christ, in whom alone we can approach to Thee."

Confession for family sins. Confess the depravity of our nature, then actual sins — especially daily sins and family sins. Recognize the punishment we deserve at the hands of a holy God, and ask God to forgive all your sins for Christ's sake.

Petition for family mercies. Ask God to deliver us from sin and evil. You might say, "O Lord, forgive our sins through Thy Son. Subdue our iniquities by Thy Spirit. Deliver us from the natural darkness of our own minds and the corruption of our own hearts. Free us from the temptations to which we were exposed today."

Ask God for temporal and spiritual good. Pray for His provision for every need in daily life. Pray for spiritual blessings. Pray that your souls are prepared for eternity.

Remember family needs, and intercede for family friends. Remember to pray in all these petitions that God's will be done. But don't allow that subjection to God's will stop you from pleading with God. Plead with Him to hear your petitions. Plead for everyone in your family as they travel to eternity. Plead for them on the basis of God's mercy, His covenant relation with you, and upon the sacrifice of Christ.

Thanksgiving as a family. Thank the Lord for food and drink, providential mercies, spiritual opportunities, answered prayers, returned health, and deliverance from evil. Confess, "It is of Thy mercies that we are not consumed as family." Remember Question 116 of the Heidelberg Catechism, which says, "God will give His grace and Holy Spirit to those only, who with sincere desires continually ask them of Him, and are thankful for them."[8]

Conclusion. Bless God for who He is and for what He has done. Ask that His kingdom, power, and glory be forever displayed. Then conclude with "Amen," which means "certainly it shall be so."

Matthew Henry said that the morning family worship is especially a time of praise and of petition for strength for the day and for divine benediction on its activities. The evening worship should focus on thankfulness, penitent reflections, and humble supplications for the night.[9]

4. For singing

- *Sing doctrinally pure songs.* There is no excuse for singing doctrinal error no matter how attractive the tune might be.

- *Sing psalms first and foremost without neglecting sound hymns.* Remember that the Psalms, called by Calvin "an anatomy of all parts of the soul," are the richest gold mine of deep, living,

---

8. *Doctrinal Standards, Liturgy, and Church Order* (Grand Rapids: Reformation Heritage Books, 1999), p. 81.

9. "A Church in the House, a Sermon Concerning Family Religion," in *The Works of Matthew Henry* (reprint Grand Rapids: Baker, 1978), 1:248–67. Cf. Thomas Doolittle, "How may the Duty of Daily Family Prayer be best managed for the Spiritual Benefit of Every One in the Family?" in *Puritan Sermons 1659–1689* (reprint Wheaton: Richard Owen Roberts, 1981), 2:194–271.

experiential scriptural piety available to us still today.

* *Sing simple psalms*, if you have young children. In choosing Psalms to sing, look for songs that children can easily master, and songs of particular importance for them to know. Choose songs that express the spiritual needs of your children for repentance, faith, and renewal of heart and life; songs that reveal God's love for His people, and the love of Christ for the lambs of His flock; or that remind them of their covenant privileges and duty. The words should be simple and plain, and the tune easy to sing. For example, in *The Psalter* see No. 53, "The Lord's My Shepherd, I'll Not Want." The text is simple enough for any child who has learned to talk; there are only three words of more than two syllables (righteousness, overflows, forevermore). Words such as righteousness, goodness, and mercy should be pointed out and explained before hand. Don't forget to begin by telling the children that a shepherd is someone who takes care of the sheep he owns and loves! It is unwise to assume that such things are plain enough in themselves.[10]

* *Sing heartily and with feeling.* As Colossians 3:23 says, "And whatsoever ye do, do it heartily,

---

10. Other suggested texts include Nos. 7; 10; 24; 30; 49; 56; 60; 140; 141; 162; 197; 200; 203; 215; 235; 246; 266; 268; 281; 287; 315; 322; 345; 362; 394; 408; 425; 431.

as to the Lord, and not unto men." Meditate on the words you are singing. On occasion discuss a phrase that is sung.

After Family Worship

As you retire for the night, pray for God's blessing on family worship: "Lord, use the instruction to save our children and to cause them to grow in grace that they might put their hope in Thee. Use our praise of Thy name in song to endear Thy name, Thy Son, and Thy Spirit to their never-dying souls. Use our stammering prayers to bring our children to repentance. Lord Jesus Christ, breathe upon our family during this time of worship with Thy Word and Spirit. Make these life-giving times."

Objections Against Family Worship 4

Some people object to regular times of family worship, citing these reasons:

- *There is no explicit command in the Bible to have family worship.* Though there is no explicit command, the texts cited earlier make clear that God would have families worship Him daily.

- *Our family doesn't have time for this.* If you have time for recreations and pleasures but no time for family worship, think about 2 Timothy 3:4–5, which warns about people who love pleasures more than God; they have a form of godliness, but deny the power of it. Time taken from family activity and business to seek God's blessing is never wasted. If we take God's Word seriously, we will say: "I can't afford not to give God and His Word priority in my family." Samuel Davies once said: "Were you formed for this world only, there would be some force in this objection, but how strange does such an objection sound coming from an heir of eternity! Pray, what is your time given to you for? Is it not principally that you may prepare for eternity? And have you no time for what is the greatest business of your lives?"[1]

◆ *There is no regular time when all of us can be together.* If you have conflicting schedules—particularly when older children are in college—you should do the best you can. Don't cancel family worship if some children are not home. Have family worship when most family members are present. If conflicts in scheduling arise, change or cancel the activity that threatens worship, if possible.

Family worship should be a non-negotiable event. Business, hobbies, sports, and school activities are secondary to family worship.

◆ *Our family is too small.* Richard Baxter said that to form a family, you only need one who governs and one who is governed. You only need two for family worship. As Jesus said, "Where two or three are gathered together in my name, there am I in the midst of them" (Matt. 18:20).

◆ *Our family is too diverse for everyone to profit.* Have a plan that covers all ages. Read a few minutes from a Bible story book for the little ones, apply a proverb for the older ones, and read a page or two from a book for teens. A wise plan can overcome any diversity of age.

---

1. "The Necessity and Excellence of Family Religion," in *Sermons on Important Subjects* (New York: Robert Carter and Brothers, 1853), p. 60.

Besides, this variation in children only directly affects about a third of family worship; it doesn't affect praying and singing. All age groups can sing and pray together. Then, too, remember that biblical instruction doesn't have to directly apply to everyone present. As you teach older teens, little children are learning to sit still. Don't continue discussion too long, however, or you'll lose everyone's interest. If the teens want to go on, resume discussion after you close in prayer and dismiss the younger ones.

Likewise, while you're teaching younger children, older teenagers are listening in. They're also learning by example how to teach younger children. When they marry and have children, they will remember how you led family worship.

♦ *I'm not good at leading our family in worship.* Here are a few suggestions. First, read a book or two on family worship, such as those written by James W. Alexander, Matthew Henry, John Howe, George Whitefield, Douglas Kelly, and Jerry Marcellino.[2] Make good use of Terry L. Johnson's *The Family Worship Book: A Resource Book for Family Devotions.*[3] Second, ask

---

2. Howe, "The Obligations from Nature and Revelation to Family Religion and Worship, represented and pressed in Six Sermons," in *The Works of John Howe* (New York: Robert Carter, 1875), 1:608–628; Whitefield, "The Great Duty of Family Religion," *The Banner of Sovereign Grace Truth* 2 (Apr-May, 1994):88–89, 120–21.

3. Fearn, Ross-shire: Christian Focus, 1998.

for guidance from God-fearing pastors and fathers. Ask if they can visit your home and either show you how to lead family worship, or observe how you do it and make suggestions. Third, start simply. I trust you are already reading Scripture and praying together. If not, begin to do so. If you are reading and praying together, add one or two questions on the portion read and sing a few psalms or hymns. Add a minute or two each week until you are up to twenty minutes.

Your skill will increase with practice. As George Whitefield said: "Where the heart is rightly disposed, it doth not demand any uncommon abilities to discharge family worship in a decent and edifying manner."[4]

Most importantly, ask the Holy Spirit to show you how. Then, out of the abundance of the heart, your mouth will speak. As Proverbs 16:23 says, "The heart of the wise teacheth his mouth, and addeth learning to his lips."

Could it be that our real problem in family worship is not our inability to pray, read, and instruct so much as our lack of grasping the astounding promises and power God has given us to shape His covenant children for His glory?

- *Some of our family members won't participate.* There may be homes in which it is difficult to

---

4. Whitefield, "The Great Duty of Family Religion," *The Banner of Sovereign Grace Truth* 2 (Apr-May, 1994):88–89, 120–21.

hold family worship. Such cases are rare, however. If you have difficult children, follow a simple rule: no Scripture, no singing, and no praying means no food. Say, "In this house, we will serve the Lord. We all breathe, therefore every person in our home must praise the Lord." Psalm 150:6 makes no such exception, even for unconverted children. It says, "Let every thing that hath breath praise the LORD. Praise ye the LORD."

- *We don't want to make hypocrites of our unconverted children.* One sin doesn't justify another. The mindset that offers this objection is dangerous. An unconverted person may never plead an unconverted state to neglect duty. Don't encourage your children to use this excuse for avoiding family worship. Stress their need to use every means of grace.

- *I can't carry a tune.* Encourage your children to learn to play the piano or organ. Or put some psalms or hymns on a tape, type out the words of the tape, and work through the tape with your family.

  The Reformers were strong on using music. Luther said, "He who does not find the gift and perfect wisdom of God in His wonderful works of music, is truly a clod, and is not worthy to be considered a man."[5]

---

5. Alexander, *Thoughts on Family Worship*, chap. 18.

Motivations for Family Worship ⑤

Every God-fearing father and mother should establish and maintain family worship in the home for the following reasons:

- *The eternal welfare of your loved ones.* God uses means to save souls. Most commonly He uses the preaching of His Word. But He may also use family worship. Like the connection between preaching and the salvation of souls in the congregation, there is a connection between family worship and the salvation of souls. Proverbs 22:6 says, "Train up a child in the way he should go: and when he is old, he will not depart from it." That rule has been confirmed for centuries. Likewise, Psalm 78:5–7 says, "For he established a testimony in Jacob, and appointed a law in Israel, which he commanded our fathers, that they should make them [i.e. the praises of the Lord and His wonderful works] known to their children: that the generation to come might know them, even the children which should be born; who should arise and declare them to their children."

We don't know the secret will of God, but we do know that God binds Himself to the means. We are called to labor in hope, making diligent use of the means of family worship, that our children may not forget the works of God. By contrast, if we leave our children to themselves, Scripture says, they will bring us to shame. The thought of children spending eternity in hell must be overwhelming to any God-fearing parent. Imagine also facing eternity confessing that we have not seriously labored for the souls of our children. It would be dreadful to confess: "I read the Bible to our children, but never talked to them about it; I prayed, but never earnestly for their souls"!

Spurgeon clearly remembered his mother tearfully praying over him like this: "Lord, Thou knowest if these prayers are not answered in Charles's conversion, these very prayers will bear witness against him in the Judgment Day." Spurgeon wrote: "The thought that my mother's prayers would serve as witness against me in the day of judgment sent terror into my heart."

Fathers, use every means to have your children snatched as brands from the burning. Pray with them, teach them, sing with them, weep over them, admonish them, plead with them and upon their baptism. Remember that at every family worship you are ushering your children into the very presence of the Most High. Seek grace to bring down the benediction of Almighty God upon your household.

• *The satisfaction of a good conscience.* Ryle said, "I charge you, fathers, take every pain to train your children in the way they should go. I charge you not merely for the sake of your children's souls; I charge you for the sake of your own future comfort and peace. Truly your own happiness in great measure depends on it. Children have caused the saddest tears that man has ever had to shed."[1] Such sorrows are heavy enough when fathers have faithfully discharged their duty yet still live with a prodigal son or daughter. But who can bear the reproach of a stinging conscience that condemns us because we never brought them up in the fear of the Lord? What shame to have failed to take seriously the vow we uttered at our children's baptism to raise our children in our confessional doctrines.

How much better if we can say: "Son, we taught you God's Word; we wrestled for your soul; we lived a God-fearing example before you. You didn't see in us a sinless piety but an unfeigned faith. You know we sought first the kingdom of God and His righteousness. Your conscience will bear witness that Christ is the center of this

---

1. *The Duties of Parents*, pp. 36–37.

home. We sang together, prayed together, and talked together. If you turn away from this light and these privileges, and insist on going your own way, we can only pray that all your Bible study, praying, and singing will not rise up against you in the Judgment Day—and that you will come to your senses before it is too late."[2]

As Ryle said, "Happy indeed is the father who can say with Robert Bolton on his deathbed to his children: 'I do believe that not one of you will dare to meet me at the tribunal of Christ in an unregenerate state.'"[3] We must so live and conduct family worship that our children will not be able to say, "I am being bound hand and foot, and being cast away into everlasting darkness because of your parental carelessness, your hypocrisy, your complacency about the things of God. Father, mother, why weren't you faithful to me?"

♦ *Assistance in child-rearing.* Family worship helps promote family harmony in times of affliction, sickness, and death. It offers greater knowledge of the Scriptures and growth in personal piety both for yourself and your children. It nurtures wisdom in how to face life, openness to speak about meaningful questions, and a closer relationship between father and children. Strong

---

2. Cf. *The Works of Matthew Henry,* 1:252.

3. *The Duties of Parents,* p. 36.

bonds established in family worship in early years may be a great help to teens in years to come. These teens may be spared from much sin when recalling family prayers and worship. In times of temptation, they may say: "How can I offend a father who daily wrestles with God on my behalf?"

J. W. Alexander advised: "Let your child enter upon adolescence and all your words will prove like a spider's web unless you shall have maintained your influence upon them by the daily growing bond of family religion. Look around you among families professing faith in Christ, and observe the difference between those who worship God and those who worship Him not; and then, as you love your offspring, and as you would save them from the rebellion of Hophni and Phinehas, set up the worship of God in your house."[4]

- *The shortness of time.* "For what is your life? It is even a vapour, that appeareth for a little time, and then vanisheth away" (James 4:14). Daily training is only for a mere twenty years or less, and even those years are not guaranteed. We ought to conduct family worship in the awareness of how brief life is in terms of never-ending eternity. Children will sense this reality if family worship is done with earnestness, love, warmth, and consistency.

---

4. Alexander, *Thoughts on Family Worship*, p. 238.

- *Love for God and His church.* Godly parents want to glorify God and serve His church. They want to give the church spiritually stalwart sons and daughters. Pray that your sons and daughters may be pillars in the church. Blessed are the parents who can one day see among the crowd of worshipers their own sons and daughters. Family worship is the foundation of such a future.

We as heads of households are accountable for the spiritual upbringing of our families. We must do everything that we can to establish and maintain family worship in our homes.

We have been given biblical examples of family worship—will we not follow them? Has God placed in our homes the souls of creatures made in His image, and will we not use all of our abilities to see our children bow in worship before God and His Son, Jesus Christ? Will we not strive to promote the Christ-centered piety in our home that family worship is so well-suited to promote? Will we trifle with the spiritual nurture, yes, with the eternity of our own family members?

Regular family worship will make our homes a more blessed place to live. It will make them more harmonious, more holy. It will help them honor God. As 1 Samuel 2:30 says, "Them that honour me I will honour, and they that despise me shall be lightly esteemed." Family worship will give us peace. It will build up the church. So, along with Joshua, we must say, "As for me and my house, we will serve the Lord.

We will use the Word to teach our children; we will daily call upon His Name; we will sing His praise with humility and joy."

If your children are grown and out of our home, it is still not too late to do the following:

- Pray for them. Pray that God may make crooked sticks straight and bring good out of evil.

- Confess your sin to God and to your children. Give them sound literature on family worship.

- Speak to and pray with your grandchildren. Do for them what you didn't do for your children.

- Begin family worship with your spouse. Follow the advice of James W. Alexander, "Fly at once, with your household, to the throne of grace."[5]

- Do not become discouraged and give up family worship, no matter what happens. Start over afresh. Press forward. Be realistic. Don't expect perfection from your efforts or your children's responses. All your perfection is in your great High Priest, who intercedes for you and has promised to be gracious to believers and their seed.

- Beg the Lord to bless your feeble efforts and save your children and grandchildren. Plead with Him to take them in His arms for all eternity. May God graciously grant His Spirit to assist you, for the good of souls, and for His name's sake.

---

5. Ibid., p. 245.

APPENDIX 1

The Directory for Family Worship[1]

Assembly at Edinburgh,
August 24, 1647

Directions for secret and private worship and mutual edification, and for censuring those who neglect family worship.

The General Assembly, after mature deliberation, approves the following rules and directions for cherishing piety and preventing division and schism. It also appoints ministers and ruling elders in each congregation to take special care that these directions are observed and followed. Likewise, presbyteries and provincial synods are to inquire and investigate whether these directions are properly observed in their jurisdictions, and they are to reprove or censure (according to the seriousness of the offence)

---

1. This edition of the Directory has been updated for the modern reader. For an annotated version of the document, giving cross-references to Scripture and the Westminster Standards, see *The Directory for Family Worship* (Greenville: Greenville Presbyterian Theological Seminary, 1994). For a commentary and study guide, see Douglas W. Comin, *Returning to the Family Altar* (Aberdeen: James Begg Society, 2004).

where necessary. So that these directions may not be rendered ineffective and unprofitable among some through the habitual neglect of the very substance of the duty of family worship, the Assembly further requires and appoints ministers and ruling elders to search and inquire diligently, in the congregations committed to their charge, whether any family among them is habitually neglecting this necessary duty. If any such family is found, the head of the family is to be first admonished privately to amend his fault. If he continues to be negligent, he is to be gravely and solemnly reproved by the session. If he still neglects family worship, for his obstinacy in such an offence he is to be suspended and debarred from the Lord's Supper, being rightly regarded as unworthy of participation in the sacrament until he rectifies the situation.

DIRECTIONS OF THE GENERAL ASSEMBLY CONCERNING SECRET AND PRIVATE WORSHIP AND MUTUAL EDIFICATION, FOR CHERISHING PIETY, FOR MAINTAINING UNITY, AND FOR AVOIDING SCHISM AND DIVISION

Besides public worship in congregations, which has been mercifully established in this land in great purity, it is expedient and necessary that secret worship by each person alone, and private worship by families, should be urged and established so that, with national reformation, the profession and power of personal and domestic godliness should be advanced.

I. First, for secret worship, it is most necessary that everyone should be devoted to prayer and meditation individually and by themselves. The unspeakable benefit is best known to those who have the most practice in this matter. Secret worship is the means whereby, in a special way, communion with God is maintained and right preparation for all other duties is obtained. Therefore, it is not only important for pastors, within their various charges, to urge individuals of all sorts to perform this duty morning and evening and at other occasions; it is also incumbent on the heads of all families to take care that they and all within their charge are diligent in these matters daily.

II. The ordinary duties included under the exercise of piety that should occur when families are convened for that purpose are these: First, prayer and praises performed with special reference to the public condition of the church of God and this kingdom, and to the present case of the family and each of its members. Next, reading of the Scriptures, with catechizing in a plain way, so that the less advanced individuals may better understand the public ordinances and Scripture reading. There should also be godly discussion that edifies all the family members in the most holy faith and includes admonition and rebuke, where appropriate, from those who have authority in the family.

III. Just as the charge and office of interpreting the Holy Scriptures is a part of the ministerial calling, and no one anywhere (however otherwise qualified) should take these responsibilities upon himself unless he is duly called by God and His church, so in every family where there is anyone who can read, the Holy Scriptures should ordinarily be read to the family. It is commendable afterwards for the family to discuss and make good use of what was read. For example, if the reading pertains to reproof against some sin, this portion may be used to make all the family careful and aware about that kind of sin. If the Scripture reading pertains to any judgment that is threatened or inflicted, it may be used to make all the family fear lest the same or a worse judgment should befall them if they do not avoid the sin that caused the judgment. Finally, if any duty is required or any comfort is held forth in a promise, the family members may be stirred up to employ Christ for strength for doing the commanded duty and to apply the offered comfort. The head of the family is to have the chief hand in all of these matters, and any member of the family may propose a question or a doubt for resolution.

IV. The head of the family is to take care that no member of the family withdraws himself from any part of family worship. Since the ordinary performance of all the parts of family worship belong properly to the head of the family, the minister is to stir up those who are lazy and train up those who are weak, so that they are fit for these exercises. It is always permissible to invite one approved by the presbytery for performing family worship. And in other families, where the head of the family is unfit, another permanent resident in the family may be approved by the minister and session to undertake that service; in such a case, the minister and session are to be accountable to the presbytery. And if a minister, by divine Providence, is brought to any family, he must never convene a part of the family for worship while secluding the rest, except in exceptional cases especially concerning these parties, which in Christian prudence need not, or ought not, to be imparted to others.

V. No idler, who has no particular calling, and no vagrant person who pretends to have a calling is permitted to perform worship in families, because people full of errors or intent on division may be ready to creep into houses and lead silly and unstable souls captive by this means.

VI. At family worship, special care is to be taken that each family keep by themselves. They should not require, invite, or admit members from other families, except for those who are lodged with them, who are at meals, or who are otherwise with them on some lawful occasion.

VII. Although there may have been effects and results of meetings of persons of various families in the times of corruption or trouble (in which cases many things are commendable that otherwise are not tolerable), yet, when God has blessed us with peace and purity of the gospel, such meetings of persons of various families (except in cases mentioned in these directions) are to be disapproved, as tending to the hindrance of the religious exercise of each family by itself, to the prejudice of the public ministry, to the tearing apart of the families of particular congregations, and, in the course of time, of the whole church. In addition, many offences may come by such a practice, resulting in the hardening of the hearts of carnal men and in the grief of the godly.

VIII. On the Lord's Day, after every one of the family individually and the whole family together have sought the Lord (in whose hands is the preparation of men's hearts) to fit them for the public worship, and to bless to them the public ordinances, the head of the family ought to see that everyone in his charge goes to public worship, so that he and they may join with the rest of the congregation. When the public worship is finished, after prayer, he should take an account of what they have heard. Afterward, they should spend the rest of the time they may spare in catechizing and in spiritual discussions of the Word of God. Alternatively, they ought to apply themselves individually to reading, meditation, and secret prayer, so that they may confirm and increase their communion with God, in order that the profit they derived from the public ordinances may be cherished and promoted, and in order that they may be more edified unto eternal life.

IX. Whoever can pray ought to make use of that gift of God. Those who are inexperienced and weaker may begin with a set form of prayer, but so that they may not be sluggish in stirring up in themselves (according to their daily necessities) the spirit of prayer, which is given to all the children of God in some measure, they ought to be more fervent and frequent in secret prayer to God, in order to enable their hearts to conceive and their tongues to express suitable desires to God for their family. In the meantime, for their greater encouragement, they should meditate on and make use of the following items of prayer.

- They should confess to God how unworthy they are to come into His presence and how unfit they are to worship His Majesty; therefore, they should earnestly ask God for the spirit of prayer.

- They should confess their sins and the sins of the family, accusing, judging, and condemning themselves for them, until they bring their souls to some measure of true humiliation.

- They should pour out their souls to God, in the name of Christ, by the Spirit, for forgiveness of sins; for grace to repent, to believe, and to live soberly, righteously, and godly; and that they may serve God with joy and delight, walking before Him.

- They should give thanks to God for His many mercies to His people, and to themselves, and especially for His love in Christ and for the light of the gospel.

- They should pray for whatever particular benefits—spiritual and temporal—they may need at that time (whether it be morning or evening), concerning health or sickness, prosperity or adversity.

- They ought to pray for the church of Christ in general, for all the Reformed churches, and for their own church in particular, and for all who suffer for the name of Christ; for all our superiors, the king's majesty, the queen, and their children; for the officers, ministers, and whole body of the congregation whereof they are members, as well as for their neighbors who are absent because of lawful undertakings, and for those who are at home.

- The prayer may be closed with an earnest desire that God may be glorified in the coming of the kingdom of His Son and in the doing of His will, and with assurance that they themselves are accepted and what they have asked according to His will shall be done.

X. These exercises ought to be performed in great sincerity, without delay, laying aside all attention to worldly business or hindrances, despite the mockings of atheists and profane men, in respect of the great mercies of God on this land and of His severe corrections with which He lately has disciplined us. And, to this effect, persons of eminence (and all elders of the church) not only ought to stir up themselves and their families to diligence in this matter, but they ought also to see to it that in all other families in which they have power and charge, the above exercises are conscientiously performed.

XI. Besides the ordinary duties in families mentioned above, there are extraordinary duties of humiliation and thanksgiving that are to be carefully performed in families on extraordinary occasions, private or public, when the Lord calls for them.

XII. Since the Word of God requires that we consider one another to provoke unto love and good works, therefore, at all times, and especially in this time, when profanity abounds and mockers, walking after their own lusts, think it is strange that others do not run with them to the same excess of riot, every member of this church ought to stir up themselves and one another to the duties of mutual edification by instruction, admonition, and rebuke. The members ought to exhort one another to manifest the grace of God in denying ungodliness and worldly lusts, and in living godly, soberly, and righteously in this present world. They ought to comfort the feeble-minded and pray with or for one another. These duties are to be performed on special occasions offered by divine providence — that is, when they are under any calamity, cross, or great difficulty, or when counsel or comfort is sought. They should perform these duties when an offender is to be reclaimed by private admonition, and if that is not effectual, one or two more should join in the admonition, according to the rule of Christ, so that in the mouth of two or three witnesses every word may be established.

XIII. Because it is not given to everyone to speak a word in season to a wearied or distressed conscience, it is expedient, in that case, that a person who finds no relief after the use of all ordinary means, private and public, should seek counsel from his or her own pastor, or some experienced Christian. If the person who is troubled in conscience is of such a condition or sex that discretion, modesty, or fear of scandal requires a godly, grave, and secret friend to be present with him or her in meeting with the pastor, it is expedient that such a friend should be present.

XIV. When people of various families are brought together by divine providence when they travel for their particular vocations or on any necessary occasions, since they desire to have the Lord their God with them wherever they go, they ought to walk with God and not neglect the duties of prayer and thanksgiving, but take care that these duties are performed by whoever the company shall determine is the most appropriate. They should likewise take heed that no corrupt communication proceeds out of their mouths, but that which is good, to the use of edifying, that it may minister grace to the hearers.

The purpose and scope of all these directions is, on the one hand, that the power and practice of godliness among all the ministers and members of this church, according to their several places and vocations, may be cherished and advanced and all impiety and mocking of religious exercises suppressed, and, on the other hand, that, under the name and pretext of religious exercises, no meetings or practices should be allowed that might breed error, scandal, schism, contempt, or misregard of the public ordinances and ministers, or neglect of the duties of particular callings, or other evils that are the works of the flesh and not of the Spirit, and are contrary to truth and peace.

John Paton Leaving Home

In case you are still questioning the impact of family worship, and to encourage fathers who are engaged in leading family worship, I wish to share with you the story of John Paton leaving home. He is leaving home for school, and from there he would become a missionary to cannibals. Paton writes:

> My dear father walked with me for the first six miles of the way. His counsels and tears and heavenly conversation on that parting journey are fresh in my heart as if it had been but yesterday; and tears are on my cheeks as freely now as then, whenever memory steals me away to the scene. For the last half-mile or so we walked on together in almost unbroken silence,—my father, as was often his custom, carrying hat in hand…. His lips kept moving in silent prayers for me; and his tears fell fast when our eyes met each other in looks for which all speech was vain! We halted on reaching the appointed parting place; he grasped my hand firmly for a minute in silence, and then solemnly and affectionately said: "God bless you, son! Your father's God prosper you, and keep you from all evil!"
>
> Unable to say more, his lips kept moving in silent prayer; in tears we embraced, and parted. I ran off as fast as I could; and, when about to turn a corner in the road where he would lose sight of

me, I looked back and saw him still standing with head uncovered where I left him—gazing after me. Waving my hat in adieu, I was around the corner in an instant. But my heart was too full and sore to carry me further, so I darted into the side of the road and wept for a time. Then, rising up cautiously, I climbed the dyke to see if he yet stood where I had left him; and just at that moment I caught a glimpse of him climbing the dyke and looking out for me! He did not see me, and after he had gazed eagerly in my direction for a while he got down, set his face towards home, and began to return—his head still uncovered, and his heart, I felt sure, still rising in prayers for me. I watched through blinding tears, till his form faded from my gaze; and then, hastening on my way, vowed deeply and oft, by the help of God, to live and act so as never to grieve or dishonour such a father and mother as He had given me. The appearance of my father, when we parted—his advice, prayers, and tears—the road, the dyke, the climbing up on it and then walking way, head uncovered—have often, often, all through life, risen vividly before my mind, and do so now while I am writing, as if it had been but an hour ago. In my earlier years particularly, when exposed to many temptations, his parting form rose before me as that of a guardian Angel. It is no Pharisaism, but deep gratitude, which makes me here testify that the memory of that scene not only helped, by God's grace, to keep me pure from prevailing sins, but also stimulated me in all my studies, that I might not fall short of his hopes, and in all my Christian duties, that I might faithfully follow his shining example.[1]

What was the underlying motivation that led John Paton to love his father and his faith so much? Paton answers:

How much my father's prayers at this time impressed me I can never explain, nor could any stranger understand. When, on his knees and all of us kneeling around him in Family Worship, he poured out his whole soul with tears for the conversion of the Heathen World to the service of Jesus, and for every personal and domestic need, we all felt as if in the presence of the living Saviour, and learned to know and love Him as our Divine Friend. As we rose from our knees, I used to look at the light on my father's face, and wish I were like him in spirit,—hoping that, in answer to his prayers, I might be privileged and prepared to carry the blessed Gospel to some portion of the Heathen World.[2]

With such a father as this, are you surprised that John Paton went to the cannibals? His wife and child would die on the mission field, where he would bury them in the sand and sleep on their graves to protect their bodies from the cannibals. Oh, the power of God-fearing family worship!

---

1. *John G. Paton: Missionary to the New Hebrides* (Edinburgh: The Banner of Truth Trust, 1965), 25–26.

2. Ibid., 21.

Scripture Index

Recommended Materials for Training Your Children in the Ways of the Lord

A QUALITY CATECHISM PROGRAM

The following list of books forms our recommemded curriculum that aims to equip families, churches, and schools with quality resources for teaching Reformed theology. This program is tailored to address every age group of our children with sound, biblical truth. Teachers' manuals are available for each of these titles.

Bible Questions and Answers:
A First Catechism
(grades K–1) by Carine Mackenzie

The Truths of God's Word:
A Student Catechism
(grades 2–3) by Joel R. Beeke and Diana Kleyn

Bible Doctrine for Younger Children 2 vol. set
(grades 4–5) by James W. Beeke

Bible Doctrine for Older Children 2 vol. set
(grades 6–7) by James W. Beeke

Bible Doctrine for Teens 3 vol. set
(grades 8–12) by James W. Beeke

DEVOTIONAL MATERIAL

These materials provide useful aids to your family devotions through short children's stories aimed at illustrating biblical truth.

God's Alphabet for Life: Devotions for Young Children

(ages 4–9)

by Joel R. Beeke and Heidi Boorsma

Using the alphabet as a guide, this book provides 26 devotional meditations for young children, based on Bible texts that children can easily memorize.

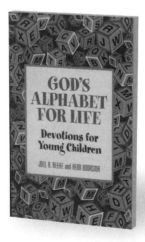

BUILDING ON THE ROCK SERIES
(ages 6–12)
by Joel R. Beeke and Diana Kleyn

Vol. 1 – How God Used a Thunderstorm
Themes: Virtuous Living and the Value of Scripture
Paperback, 145 pages

Vol. 2 – How God Stopped the Pirates
Themes: Missionary Tales and Remarkable Conversions
Paperback, 163 pages

Vol. 3 – How God Used a Snowdrift
Themes: Honoring God and Dramatic Deliverances
Paperback, 171 pages

Vol. 4 – How God Used a Drought and an Umbrella
Themes: Faithful Witnesses and Childhood Faith
Paperback, 162 pages

Vol. 5 – How God Sent a Dog to Save a Family
Themes: God's Care and Childhood Faith
Paperback, 165 pages

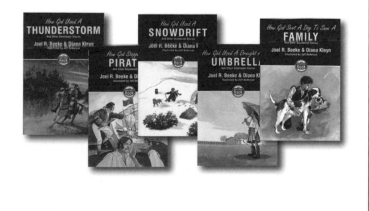

THE LORD'S GARDEN SERIES
by Diana Kleyn

VOLUME 1
Taking Root
Conversion Stories for Children

This book, designed to teach spiritual truths to children, uses the theme of plants taking root and growing in grace.

Paperback, 190 pages

VOLUME 2
Bearing Fruit
Stories about Godliness for Children

Just as trees and plants bear fruit, so must the child of God. *Bearing Fruit* shows children that Christians should be recognized by a lifestyle and walk that testifies about Jesus Christ.

Paperback, 152 pages

VOLUME 3
Sowing the Seed
Stories about Sharing the Gospel with Others

A garden will never grow unless someone takes the time to plant the seeds. These stories about missions and evangelism reinforce the importance of sharing the gospel and encourage children to see the joy of telling others about Jesus.

Paperback, 150 pages

ADDITIONAL MATERIAL USEFUL FOR FAMILY WORSHIP

Thoughts on Family Worship
by James W. Alexander
A thorough and convicting defense of family worship

365 Days with Calvin
Joel R. Beeke, ed.
Updated selections from Calvin, together
with applications by the editor

The Family Worship Book
by Terry Johnson
A helpful resource book for family devotions

From the Lips of Little Ones
by Jeff Kingswood
A study in the Westminster Shorter Catechism
"for very little people" (covered in 73 weeks)

Reformation Heroes
by Diana Kleyn with Joel R. Beeke
Forty Reformers' lives, together with illustrations
(ages 10 & up)

The Psalter
450 selections of psalm singing

Expository Thoughts on the Gospels (7 vols.)

by J. C. Ryle

Ryle presents short Scripture readings followed by two to four
lessons to learn from each reading (ages 10 & up).

History Lives (5 vols.)

by Mindy and Brandon Withrow

Engagingly covers two millenia of church history.
(ages 9–14)

All of these are available at discount prices from:
Reformation Heritage Books
2965 Leonard St., NE
Grand Rapid, MI 49525
616-977-0599 / Fax 616-285-3246
e-mail: orders@heritagebooks.org
website: www.heritagebooks.org